STEM STARS

Women Who Rocked
MEDICINE

PaRragon

Bath · New York · Cologne · Melbourne · Delhi
Hong Kong · Shenzhen · Singapore

This edition published by Parragon Books Ltd in 2017 and distributed by

Parragon Inc.
440 Park Avenue South, 13th Floor
New York, NY 10016
www.parragon.com

Written by Heather Alexander
Edited by Jeanine Le Ny
Art Direction by Andrew Barthelmes
Designed by Keith Plechaty

With thanks to Susan Lurie Ink, Inc.

Cover image of Marie Curie as portrayed by Storysmith® Susan Marie Frontczak in "The Living History of Marie Curie" courtesy of Susan Marie Frontczak and photographer, Paul Schroder.

ISBN 978-1-4748-9204-9

Printed in China

Picture Credits:
t = top, b = bottom

© Getty Images
Bettmann/Contributor/ 20t, Universal History Archive/Contributor, Bettmann/Contributor 30b, Jewel Samad/Staff 32t, Jewel Samad/Staff 32b, Dan Nalbandian/Contributor 38t, NurPhoto/Contributor 39b

© istockphoto.com
imagepointphoto 4t, skynesher 5b, tillsonburg 18b, Virtaa 20b, blueringmedia 21b, sibgat 23b, GeorgeRudy 26b, BrianAJackson 27b, from2015 29t, Clicknique 31b, ttsz 35b, FarmVeld 36b, monkeybusinessimages 37t, lisegagne 38b, Dr_Microbe 40b

© Shutterstock.com
Aleksandar Grozdanovski 13b, galaira 14t

© Creative Commons
Wellcome Library, London/CC BY 4.0 8b, 9b, 24t, 24b, 25t, USAE Savannah/CC BY 2.0 11t, The Maryland Science Center/CC BY-ND 2.0 16t, PLOS/CC BY 2.5 (cropped) 28b, John D. & Catherine T. MacArthur Foundation/CC BY 4.0 40t

Courtesy of
Dr. Maria Siemionow 42t, 42b, 43b, Library of Congress LC-USZ62-9797 6t, LC-USZC4-507 7t, LC-DIG-ppmsca-037769 8t, LCUSZ62-69290 10t, LC-USZ62-2053, LC-USZ62-131534 22t, cph3c31540 22b, U.S. National Library of Medicine 30t, 33t, 34t, 34b

Public Domain 5t, 6b, 19t, 41t, {PD-1923} 10b, 12t, 14b, 15b, 16b, 17b, 18t, {PD-USGov} 26t, 36t, 34t

Contents

Introduction

> "None of us can know what we are capable of until we are tested."
>
> —Elizabeth Blackwell

Throughout history, women have always taken care of people who are sick. They've bandaged wounds, delivered babies, made herbal remedies, and nursed families through fevers and infections. Cleopatra Metrodora, a surgeon who lived in ancient Greece, even wrote a medical book as far back as 490 CE. So, can you imagine there was a time when people thought that women *shouldn't* be doctors?

In the 1400s, long after Cleopatra Metrodora's time, governments in Europe decided that only those trained at universities could practice medicine. Back then, men made the rules. Women weren't allowed to study at universities, so they couldn't become doctors.

Then, in the late 1700s, men began to realize that women would make great nurses, since they took care of their families—but they still believed a woman could not be a doctor.

Fortunately, those mistaken ideas did not get in the way of some fearless women, such as:

- Margaret Bulkley. In the 1800s, she disguised herself as a man, became a doctor, and served in the British Army for about 50 years—as Dr. James Barry!
- And Harriet Hunt. In 1847 she was the first woman to apply to Harvard Medical School. She was turned away. What did she do? She practiced medicine *without* a license—and her waiting room in Boston was packed with patients.

No one knew Dr. James Barry was really *Margaret Bulkley*—until after she died.

For these women and others who followed, medicine was their passion. They wanted to heal and help people—to find cures and better treatments. Their determination brought about amazing breakthroughs and inventions.

The women in this book are pioneers who have paved a path for many incredible soon-to-be-women—like you and your friends—to follow their dreams and to rock the world of medicine just as they did.

Dorothea Dix

"In a world where there is so much to be done, I felt strongly impressed that there must be something for me to do." —Dorothea Dix

Dorothea Dix cared. She cared for her brothers when they were young, and later she would care for her mother and grandmother. Dorothea cared about people she didn't know, too—people who couldn't ask for help but needed it. She began speaking for them, fighting for them. And one day, Dorothea would have others caring, too.

Lessons, Lessons

Dorothea Dix was born in 1802 in Maine. Her father was a strict preacher, and her mother suffered from depression. When Dorothea was 12, she and her two younger brothers were sent to live with their grandmother in Massachusetts. Dorothea later became a teacher and opened two schools for girls—one for paying students and another for girls who couldn't pay. Then one day Dorothea was asked to teach Sunday school to some

Dorothea's work helped establish over 100 mental hospitals.

Dorothea volunteered for the Union Army, but she nursed both Union and Confederate soldiers with equal care.

women prisoners at a jail. What she learned there would turn out to be very important.

Big Changes

Dorothea saw that mentally sick people were being kept in cold and dirty, rat-filled cells at the prison. She saw women naked and hungry. Some were tied up and left to sleep on stone floors. Dorothea was horrified to learn that this happened at other places, too! She had to do something. For the next twenty years, she traveled the United States writing and talking about the cruel treatment of mentally ill people. Finally state governments listened. They improved mental hospitals and built new ones. They also took steps to begin treating those with mental illness, instead of simply locking them away.

Dorothea paused her work when the Civil War began. She volunteered to be a nurse for the Union Army. Although she had no formal medical experience, the army put her in charge of training and organizing the nurses. When the war ended, she continued her fight for the rights of mental health patients across the world until her death in 1887.

WHOA!

- Dorothea was tough. She was nicknamed "Dragon Dix" by the Union nurses because she made them follow strict rules.

- Dorothea wrote several books—including ones for kids!

Florence Nightingale

"I attribute my success to this—
I never gave or took any excuse."

—Florence Nightingale

What if your doctors and nurses never washed their instruments? Or never changed bed sheets? Or used dirty bandages? In the 1800s, hospitals were run this way, but Florence knew sick people needed clean surroundings and better care to get well. So what did she do? She pioneered changes that we still use today.

A Surprise Announcement

Florence was born in 1820 to a wealthy British family that was living in Florence, Italy. The family soon moved back to England, and her father taught her subjects most girls didn't learn in the 1800s—math, languages, science, and philosophy. Young

During the war, Florence was known as "The Lady with the Lamp" because she visited patients at night.

women at that time were expected to marry and have children. But Florence announced she didn't want to be a wife and mother. She wanted to be a nurse. Her family was not very happy.

Back then nurses were not valued. Hospitals were dirty and often scary. Florence didn't care. She trained and started working in a London hospital. In 1854, the Crimean War broke out. British soldiers were wounded and needed care. Florence traveled to Scutari (near today's Istanbul, Turkey) with a staff of 38 nurses to help. She was shocked by what she found.

Clean Up!

More soldiers were dying of infections from the dirty hospital than from their battle injuries! Florence got right to work organizing and cleaning the hospital, changing sheets, and caring for patients. She made charts that showed how keeping things clean helped soldiers get well. In fact, her methods lessened the death rate by two-thirds. By the end of the war, Florence had become famous for her care.

Back in London, Florence opened a school where she trained women—both wealthy and poor—to be nurses. She also wrote a book called *Notes on Nursing*. It was the first patient-care book the average person could understand. Florence died in 1910. She is thought of as one of the most important nurses in history.

Nurses trained at Florence's school were called "Nightingale Nurses." They shared her methods of care around the world.

Clara Barton

> "I may be compelled to face danger, but never fear it, and while our soldiers can stand and fight, I can stand and feed and nurse them."
>
> —Clara Barton

Every eight minutes the American Red Cross responds to an emergency, such as a flood, an earthquake, or a war. When disaster strikes, people in the United States and all over the world look to this important organization for medical care, blood, shelter, and relief—and it was all started by one brave woman: Clara Barton.

Taking Care of Others

Clara Barton was born in 1821, in Massachusetts. She was a shy child who loved to take care of others. When she was 11, her older brother David fell off their barn roof. David was bedridden for two years, and Clara nursed him back to health. Back then, most professional nurses were men. Teaching was one of the few jobs for women, so when Clara was a teenager, she became a teacher. She taught for 15 years.

The wounded Civil War soldiers called Clara the "Angel of the Battlefield."

Today the ARC has over 600 chapters across the country and about 500,000 volunteers.

When the Civil War started in 1861, Clara collected supplies and gave them out to the Union Army. She made bandages from sheets and towels for the wounded soldiers. But Clara wanted to do more. Instead of staying safely out of firing range, she went to the battlefield to care for soldiers herself. The work was very dangerous. Once, a bullet nicked the sleeve of her shirt, then killed the soldier she was helping!

Red Cross

After the war, Clara helped families find soldiers who were missing. She traveled to Europe and joined the International Red Cross during the Franco-Prussian War. Clara wanted to start an American Red Cross in the United States. But government leaders didn't think people needed a relief organization if the country wasn't at war. Clara didn't take no for an answer. She showed them that it was important to be prepared for an emergency. In 1881 she formed the American Red Cross. She was the president of the ARC for 23 years. Clara died in 1912, but the American Red Cross continues to help people every day.

WHOA!

The American Red Cross . . .

- Helps people hurt by disasters.
- Supports the military and their families.
- Supplies blood to many hospitals.
- Educates on health and safety.
- Helps other countries that need relief, too!

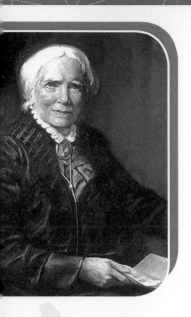

> ## "It is not easy to be a pioneer—but, oh, it is fascinating!"
> —Elizabeth Blackwell

These days, lots of women are doctors, but it wasn't always like that. Back when Elizabeth Blackwell was a little girl, most people thought that women were not smart enough for the job. But Elizabeth knew that she was just as smart as any boy—maybe smarter. Soon the whole world would know it, too.

Smart Start

Elizabeth Blackwell was born in 1821 in Bristol, England. She had four brothers and four sisters. Unlike many parents of the time, Elizabeth's mom and dad made sure Elizabeth and her sisters were as well educated as their brothers were. Elizabeth loved learning—especially history. When she was

Elizabeth opened a hospital to care for the poor. *And* she founded a medical college for women so that others could follow in her footsteps.

11 years old, her family moved to the United States. Years later, Elizabeth became a teacher.

Mind Made Up

When Elizabeth was 24, her friend Mary got very sick. Before Mary died, she told Elizabeth how embarrassing it was to be examined by a man. Mary wished she'd had a woman for a doctor, and she begged Elizabeth to study medicine.

Elizabeth wasn't sure. After all, the sight of blood made her dizzy. But if a woman wanted a female doctor, why shouldn't she have one? So Elizabeth decided to go for it!

A woman had never gone to medical school before. Elizabeth applied to 29 schools. They all refused her except for Geneva Medical College in New York. The doctors who ran the school thought it would be funny to ask the students if a woman should be allowed to study there. As a joke, the students voted "Yes." They never thought Elizabeth would actually show up for class. Elizabeth did show up—and she graduated at the top of her class!

Elizabeth discovered that washing hands and keeping things clean stopped the spread of disease.

WHOA!

⚛ Elizabeth tried sleeping on the hard floor to make herself tougher.

⚛ True to their beliefs, Elizabeth and her family gave up sugar in protest of the slave trade.

Rebecca Lee Crumpler

"I early conceived a liking for, and sought every opportunity to relieve the sufferings of others."

—Rebecca Lee Crumpler

When Rebecca Lee Crumpler was a girl, she'd watch her aunt take care of sick people. Rebecca wanted to do the same, so she became a nurse when she grew up. Several doctors said she was smart enough to become a doctor herself. Rebecca didn't take them seriously. There were barely any female doctors in the United States and absolutely no female African-American doctors.

The New England Female Medical College was the first school to train women as doctors. Rebecca was the only African–American to attend the school. It closed in 1873.

The more she thought about it, the more she realized that someone had to be the first. Why not her?

Amazing Accomplishment

Rebecca Lee Crumpler was born in Delaware in 1831 and grew up with her aunt in Pennsylvania. She later moved to Massachusetts and went to a private school. Rebecca became a nurse during a time

Rebecca's book was dedicated to mothers, nurses, as well as anyone who wanted to help lessen people's suffering.

when it was very hard for poor African-Americans to get good health care.

Rebecca was admitted into the New England Female Medical College. In 1864, she became the first African-American woman to earn a medical degree. How incredible was this? In 1860, out of 54,543 doctors in the United States only 300 were women, and none of them were African-American. In 1920, 56 years after Rebecca became a doctor, there were still only 65 African-American women doctors in the United States.

Helping the Poor and Forgotten

Rebecca moved to Richmond, Virginia, at the end of the Civil War. Rebecca gave medical care to newly freed slaves. She was one of the first doctors to help this often-forgotten group, and she didn't ask for payment. After 15 years, she moved north to Boston. There, she was a doctor to women, children, and the poor. In 1883, she wrote a book called *A Book of Medical Discourses in Two Parts*. It explained how women could give themselves and their children medical care. It was one of the first medical books written by an African-American. Rebecca died in 1895.

WHOA!

⚛ What did Rebecca look like? No one knows. Not one picture of her has ever been found!

⚛ Rebecca was married twice—first to Wyatt Lee, who died, and then to Arthur Crumpler.

Marie Curie

> "I am among those who think that science has great beauty."
>
> —Marie Curie

Have you ever heard of radiation? It's energy that travels in the form of waves or really fast-moving particles. Marie Curie was the first scientist to understand how radiation works—a discovery that is saving lives to this day.

Sister Act

Marie Curie was born Maria Sklodowska in 1867 in Poland. After high school Marie wanted to go to college, but Polish universities did not take girls in the 1800s. Marie's older sister, Bronya, wanted to go, too. The Sorbonne University in Paris, France, was letting girls study there, but there wasn't enough money for both sisters to attend. Marie and Bronya came up with a plan. Bronya would go first and Marie would work to pay for it. Then Bronya would do the same for Marie. Their plan worked! Bronya became a doctor, and Marie became a scientist. Later Marie married Pierre Curie, who was a scientist, too.

The Curies invented the term "radioactivity" to describe elements that give off lots of rays. They discovered that radiation could heal cancer cells. And Marie founded the Curie Institute to research and treat cancer.

Radioactive!

Marie and Pierre spent hours in the lab together. They studied a metal called uranium. Marie discovered that it gave off rays. Then she studied a rock called pitchblende. It gave off even more rays than uranium. Why? Marie did lots of experiments. She discovered that pitchblende contained two new chemical elements. The Curies named them polonium (after Poland) and radium (because it gave off lots of rays). In 1903, Marie, Pierre, and physicist Henri Becquerel were awarded the Nobel Prize in Physics for their work on radium. Then in 1911, Marie won *another* Nobel Prize in Chemistry for discovering polonium and radium. No one had ever won two Nobel Prizes before!

WHOA!

- Marie became the first female professor to teach at the Sorbonne.

- She and Albert Einstein were friends!

- Marie's oldest daughter, Irene, won a Nobel Prize in Chemistry, too!

Her work did not stop there. When World War I started, Marie knew that doctors needed X-rays to help injured soldiers. The problem was, the machines were too big to bring to the battlefield. So, Marie invented a smaller one that could work on a truck and go anywhere. In 1934, Marie died from being around too much radiation. At that time, no one knew it was dangerous. Today doctors and scientists know how to use radiation safely.

The trucks that carried X-ray machines were called "little Curies." During World War I, Marie would often take the machines to the battlefields herself!

Susan La Flesche Picotte

"My office hours are any and all hours of the day and night."

—Susan La Flesche Picotte

Susan La Flesche Picotte was a Native American who grew up on the Omaha Indian Reservation in Nebraska. When Susan was a girl, she tried to help a sick woman on the reservation. She sent for the white doctor four times, but he wouldn't come. The woman died in pain. How could a doctor refuse to help? Something needed to change. Her people needed their own doctor—one who would never say no. Susan was ready for the challenge.

First Doctor

Susan La Flesche Picotte was born in 1865. She was the youngest daughter of Chief Joseph La Flesche ("Iron Eyes") of the Omaha tribe and Mary Gale ("One Woman"). Her parents were

Susan kept a lit lantern in her window at night to signal that she would help at all hours.

of mixed ancestry. They wanted her to live in both the white and Native American worlds, so they sent her off the reservation to go to school. After high school, Susan attended the Women's Medical College of Pennsylvania, one of the few medical schools

The Susan La Flesche Picotte Memorial Hospital was built in 1912. The hospital was named a National Historic Landmark in 1993.

that accepted women at the time. Her favorite class was human anatomy. Susan was the first Native American woman to become a physician.

Horse and Buggy House Calls

In 1889, Susan returned to Nebraska and set up her doctor's office. She treated Native Americans and many white patients, too. Her patients were scattered across hundreds of miles with very few roads. They were poor and sick with tuberculosis, smallpox, measles, and influenza. During the harsh winter of 1891, Susan cared for more than 100 patients a month. Pulled in a buggy by her horse, Pie, Susan would travel for miles through freezing blizzards to see her patients.

In 1894, she married Henry Picotte, and they had two children. Later, Susan opened the first hospital on the Omaha Reservation. She educated tribal people on how diseases spread as well as the benefits of fresh air and getting rid of trash. Often in poor health herself, Susan died in 1915.

WHOA!

⚛ Susan was born in a buffalo-hide teepee.

⚛ When medical supplies on the reservation ran out, Susan would often use her own money to buy more.

⚛ Susan was also an activist. She wrote letters and met with government leaders to fight for the rights of her people.

"Learn to listen with your fingers."

—Helen Taussig

One day Helen Taussig noticed she was having trouble hearing. A doctor told her the bad news—she'd be deaf very soon. Helen was a doctor, too, a children's heart doctor. She needed to be able to hear her patients' heartbeats. Was her career over? Not at all!

Keep Going

Helen Taussig was born in 1898 in Cambridge, Massachusetts. Her father was an economics professor at Harvard University, and her mother was one of the first women to graduate Radcliffe College. That didn't mean Helen's childhood was easy, though. Helen was smart, but she suffered from dyslexia, and she had trouble reading. Her father tutored her for hours every day after school. When Helen was 11, her mom died from tuberculosis, and Helen later caught the disease, too. But she wouldn't let anything stop her. Helen graduated college and received her medical degree from Johns Hopkins University in Baltimore.

Helen was the first woman elected president of the American Heart Association.

By the time she graduated, Helen had lost her hearing. She specialized in cardiology, the study of the heart, but she couldn't hear a heartbeat. Helen didn't let that stop her. She learned to press on a child's chest and feel the rhythm of the heartbeat through her fingertips. In 1930, she was named director of Hopkins' clinic for children. She was one of the first women in the country to hold such an important position.

WHOA!

- Using her sense of touch, Helen sometimes found irregular heartbeats that "hearing" doctors had missed!
- Helen received the Presidential Medal of Freedom in 1964.

L is for . . .

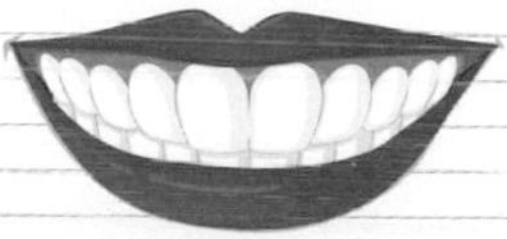

lips

Helen learned to read lips so that she could understand the needs of her patients.

"Blue Babies"

In the late 1930s, Helen began to notice that some sick babies in the clinic had a bluish tint to their skin, lips, and nails. She figured out that these "blue babies" were not pumping enough blood from their lungs to their hearts. Helen studied X-rays of their hearts and saw that a blood vessel was closed when it needed to be open. So, she developed a tiny tube called a shunt to solve the problem. It needed to be put inside the heart. This kind of heart surgery had never been done on a baby before. Helen teamed up with a heart surgeon, and they put the first shunt in a one-year-old girl in 1944. It worked! Thousands of children's lives have been saved because of Helen's groundbreaking invention.

> "Nobody, but nobody, is going to stop breathing on me!"
>
> —Virginia Apgar

Do you remember the first test you ever took? It happened right when you were born. The nurse or doctor gave the test, and you received an Apgar score. This score let them know if you needed special care. It has saved the lives of countless babies—and it was all Virginia Apgar's idea.

New Field

Born in 1909 in New Jersey, Virginia Apgar studied medicine at Columbia University. In 1933, she thought about being a surgeon but decided to be an anesthesiologist instead. An anesthesiologist makes sure a patient is comfortable during surgery. This doctor also monitors a patient's breathing and heartbeat during surgery. At the time, this was a new field. But Virginia knew it was important, especially as

Virginia was also passionate about preventing birth defects.

more difficult surgeries were being performed. In 1938, she was hired as director of the brand-new anesthesia division at Columbia University.

The Baby Test

At that time a lot of babies in the United States were dying soon after birth. This bothered Helen. Doctors were paying attention to the mother's health, which was important. But what was happening to the babies? Since she was an anesthesiologist, she realized that low oxygen caused at least half of newborn deaths. If babies in need could be given oxygen right away, many would be saved.

A medical student asked Virginia how to tell which babies were at risk. She quickly wrote down five signs: 1) heart rate, 2) breathing, 3) muscle tone or activity, 4) reflexes, and 5) color. Each of the five signs, studied at one minute and five minutes after birth, was rated 0, 1, or 2. A score of 10 meant the baby was in very good health.

The Apgar score worked. Thousands more babies survived each year. Virginia's baby scoring system is still used today all around the world.

WHOA!
Doctors today use Virginia's last name to remember what to look for:

- 🅐ppearance
- 🅟ulse
- 🅖rimace
- 🅐ctivity
- 🅡espiration

Virginia would carry a penknife and some other tools wherever she went, in case she needed to perform emergency surgery.

Gertrude Belle Elion

> "In my day women were told we didn't go into chemistry. I saw no reason why we couldn't."
>
> —Gertrude Belle Elion

When Gertrude Belle Elion started Hunter College at age 15, she needed to choose a major. She loved *all* subjects, but after her grandfather died from cancer, Gertrude picked chemistry. She wanted to find a way to stop sick people from suffering as he had. And she did just that!

Gertrude took on more responsibility at George Hitchings' lab as fast as she could.

Working for Free

Gertrude Belle Elion was born in New York City in 1918. When she was seven, her family moved near the Bronx Zoo, which she loved to visit. After graduating college, Gertrude didn't have money to go to graduate school, and she couldn't find a job in a laboratory. Then one day Gertrude met a chemist who needed an assistant, but he couldn't pay her. Gertrude decided that getting experience was worth working for free. She worked there for a year and a half. Later she earned a small salary and saved enough money to graduate from New York University. She was the only woman in the chemistry program.

Important Work Begins

After World War II started, many men had to go off to fight in the war. Companies started looking for female chemists. Gertrude was hired by a food company. She had to test pickles and to make sure that berries for the jams were not moldy. It was a fine job, but Gertrude wanted to do something bigger. In 1944, Dr. George H. Hitchings offered her a job at a drug company. Gertrude started as his assistant, and later she became the head of experimental therapy. Finally, she was in the right place!

Gertrude was the first woman to be welcomed into the National Inventors Hall of Fame.

Together George and Gertrude made drugs for diseases such as leukemia and malaria. They also made drugs to help people with kidney transplants and immune disorders. These drugs saved thousands of lives. In 1988, Gertrude won the Nobel Prize for her work—along with George and a British chemist named Sir James Black. She was the first person to receive the Nobel Prize who wasn't a doctor.

WHOA!

⚛ Gertrude held 45 patents in medicine and was awarded 23 honorary degrees.

⚛ She tried secretarial school when she couldn't get a research job. It lasted six weeks.

Jane Cooke Wright

"I know I'm a member of two minority groups, but I don't think of myself that way." —Jane Cooke Wright

The very first time Jane Cooke Wright saw a Rubik's Cube, she dropped what she was doing to twist and turn the squares. She refused to stop until she'd found the answer to the puzzle. Jane was a puzzle-solver when it came to medicine, too. She led the way in chemotherapy—a therapy using powerful drugs to kill cancer cells. It changed the treatment of cancer forever.

Family Business

Jane was co-founder of the American Society of Clinical Oncology.

In 1919, Jane Cooke Wright was born into a family of doctors in New York City. Jane's family was African-American, and most doctors back then were white. Born into slavery, her grandfather graduated from medical school after the Civil War. Her father was one of the first African-American graduates of Harvard Medical School. He was also the first African-American doctor on the staff of a New York City hospital. Jane studied art in college. Before she graduated, though, her dad had convinced her to study medicine instead.

A New Treatment

Cancer treatment has always been one of medicine's biggest puzzles. Before the 1940s, doctors used surgery or radiation to treat an area of the body that had cancer. Most blood cancers could not be cured. Jane and her dad wanted to find a way to kill cancer throughout the entire body. They studied people who had suffered mustard-gas attacks in World War II. They found that the gas destroyed a person's white blood cells. Patients with leukemia, a blood cancer, have abnormal white blood cells. So, Jane and her father began to experiment with different chemicals to kill leukemia cells. Jane tested hundreds of chemicals, first on mice then on human tissue samples. When she was that sure she had the right chemical mixture, she started treating people.

WHOA!

⚛ Jane was the first woman to serve as president of the New York Cancer Society.

⚛ Her nickname was "The Mother of Chemotherapy."

Jane became a leader in oncology, the study of cancer. In 1964, she developed a system to deliver chemotherapy to tumors in hard to reach places, such as a kidney or the liver. Before this, doctors often had to remove the entire organ to get rid of cancer tumors. Jane turned chemotherapy from an experiment into a treatment that could help people get well.

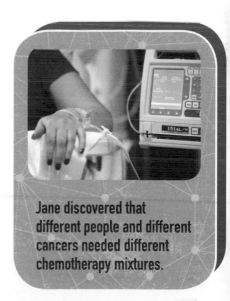

Jane discovered that different people and different cancers needed different chemotherapy mixtures.

> "Science and everyday life cannot and should not be separated."
>
> —Rosalind Franklin

Have you ever worked on a project with someone you didn't get along with? Chemist Rosalind Franklin did. She was hired to be partners with Maurice Wilkins at King's College, London. But Maurice treated her like a lower-level assistant. One day, Maurice showed Rosalind's research to other scientists. These scientists made a major discovery using her research. It won the Nobel Prize—and Rosalind was completely left out of it.

X-ray Vision

Rosalind Franklin was born in London, England, in 1920. She loved facts and logic and decided to become a scientist. In 1938, she was admitted to the University of Cambridge to study chemistry. She wanted to be a molecular biologist.

In 1951, Rosalind was one of the scientists at King's College who were trying to figure out the shape of DNA. DNA is the molecule that tells every cell

Years after they'd won the Nobel Prize, James Watson and Francis Crick admitted they never would have discovered the shape of DNA without Rosalind's research.

This is a model of what DNA looks like.

in your body what to do. Rosalind was brought on for her expertise with X-rays. She used X-rays to study the thin DNA fibers. She took a now-famous picture called photo 51, which showed that DNA was a double helix. That means it looks like a ladder twisted into a spiral. This was very important new information.

Meanwhile, Across Town . . .

Two other scientists named James Watson and Francis Crick were also trying to find out the shape of DNA. They had built a good model, but it wasn't quite right. Without asking Rosalind's permission, Maurice Wilkins showed them her X-ray photo of DNA. This filled in their missing knowledge. James and Francis published an article about the structure of DNA but never mentioned Rosalind—or told her that they'd used photo 51. She died in 1958 at the age of 37 from cancer. Four years later, Watson, Crick, and Wilkins won the Nobel Prize for their work on DNA. As a result, Rosalind Franklin is probably best known for the award she *didn't* win. But without her research and photo 51, scientists may never have cracked the "code" of what makes us who we are.

WHOA!

⚛ At first Rosalind's father refused to pay for college. He didn't think women should go! Rosalind's mother and aunt changed his mind.

⚛ Nobel prizes are awarded only to people who are alive. Rosalind's important work has been recognized, but she cannot receive a Nobel Prize.

Rosalyn Sussman Yalow

> ## "We must believe in ourselves or no one else will believe in us."
> —Rosalyn Sussman Yalow

When Rosalyn Sussman was eight years old, she announced she'd be a "big-deal" scientist when she grew up. Rosalyn was right about that—and she won the Nobel Prize to prove it!

No Stopping Her

Rosalyn Sussman was born in 1921 in New York City. In college, she became interested in physics. Most physics graduate programs did not let in women back then. Maybe she should teach elementary school instead, her parents suggested. Rosalyn said no. Then a professor offered her a job as a secretary at Columbia University's medical school, and she accepted. Her plan was to sneak into graduate classes when she wasn't working. But only a few months later, she received an offer to attend the College of Engineering at the University of Illinois— and to be an assistant teacher there, too. Many young men were fighting in World

Using RIA, Rosalyn discovered that there are two types of diabetes— Type 1: when a patient's body does not make insulin, and Type 2: when a patient's body does not use its insulin correctly.

War II at the time. The college had to invite women or risk having to close. Rosalyn jumped at the chance.

When Rosalyn arrived at the College of Engineering, she was the only woman in a group of 400 students. The last time a woman had attended the school was in 1917! In her first year, Rosalyn received an A in every class, except for an A-minus in an optics laboratory. The chairman of the Physics Department pointed to the A-minus as proof that "women do not do well in lab work." Rosalyn did not let his words stop her. She was even more determined to succeed.

WHOA!

⚛ RIA helped create the field of nuclear medicine. Doctors use nuclear medicine to look inside the body and see how it is working.

⚛ A school in the Bronx was named after Rosalyn.

RIA

Rosalyn began a career in medical research. In the 1950s, she co-discovered radioimmunoassay—or RIA for short. RIA is a test that can measure teeny things like hormones in blood. Hormones affect how the body develops and works. Rosalyn first used RIA to study insulin in patients with a disease called diabetes. Since then, doctors have been able to measure levels of other tiny things in blood such as vitamins and

Doctors need only a small amount of blood to do an RIA test.

more—all too small to measure before. RIA changed the way scientists and doctors studied disease and developed treatments and cures. In 1977, Rosalyn won a Nobel Prize for her work. She died in 2011.

Janet Rowley

> "The exhilaration that one gets in making new discoveries is beyond description."
> —Janet Rowley

Janet Rowley was so excited! She'd been accepted into the University of Chicago's medical school. Then she found out she wouldn't be able to go. Why? In 1944, the medical school allowed only three women in a class of 65, and those spots had already been filled. Janet had to wait. But finally, Janet started—and it's a good thing she did. She went on to make an amazing discovery!

Chromosome Explorer

Janet Rowley was born in New York City in 1925 then moved to Chicago. She loved to read, especially books about science. At age 15, she attended college on a special scholarship for gifted students. She graduated from medical school at age 23. After marrying and having four sons, she worked at a clinic for children with Down syndrome, a condition caused by an extra chromosome. Chromosomes are thread-like strands inside human cells. Normally, in each cell there are 23 chromosomes

Janet had said she felt humbled by winning the Presidential Medal of Freedon in 2009.

from your mother and 23 from your father for a total of 46 chromosomes. Each chromosome has genes in them. Your genes make you unique. They decide things like if you have curly or straight hair, your eye color, if you are a boy or a girl, and so on. Janet became very interested in chromosomes and genes. She traveled to the University of Oxford in England to learn new ways to study them.

An Amazing Discovery

When Janet returned to the United States, she joined a lab at the University of Chicago that was doing chromosome research on a type of cancer called leukemia. At the time, scientists didn't understand why patients with a certain kind of leukemia had one abnormally short chromosome. One day, Janet spread pictures of the chromosomes on her dining room table to take a closer look. That's when she saw it. One chromosome had swapped genes with another chromosome. The patient's body had made a genetic mistake! Janet was the first to discover that genetic mistakes could cause cancer. Janet received many awards for her work, including the National Medal of Science and the Presidential Medal of Freedom.

WHOA!

- Janet's discovery helped develop drugs that target certain kinds of cancers, helping patients live longer lives.

- Humans have about 20,000 genes. Bananas have about 30,000 genes.

> "Do not allow your mind to be imprisoned by majority thinking. Remember that the limits of science are not the limits of imagination."
>
> —Patricia Bath

Patricia Bath was a super student. She finished high school in two years. She attended a cancer research workshop, and her findings were published in a scientific paper. Soon Patricia would go on to become a doctor, teacher, and inventor who would save the sight of thousands!

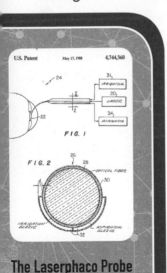

The Laserphaco Probe used a laser to vaporize cataracts by making a tiny hole in the eye.

Seeing Eye to Eye

Patricia Bath was born in 1942 in Harlem, New York. Her father was the first African-American motorman for the New York City subway system, and her mother was a domestic worker who saved her salary for her children's education. Patricia chose medicine as a career and graduated from Howard University medical school.

She trained in ophthalmology at Harlem Hospital and at Columbia University Hospital. Ophthalmology is the study of the eye. During her training, Patricia discovered that African-Americans in Harlem went blind twice as often as white Americans at nearby Columbia. This was because they did not have access to good eye care. Patricia came up with a solution: community ophthalmology. Volunteers were trained and sent to senior centers and schools to test people for eye diseases—before they showed symptoms. This care has saved the sight of many people. Community ophthalmology is now practiced around the world.

Not Done Yet!

In 1973, Patricia became the first African-American to complete a residency in ophthalmology. She then became the first female staff member in UCLA's Department of Ophthalmology. Patricia wasn't finished achieving "firsts." She invented the Laserphaco Probe, making her the first African-American female doctor to receive a patent for a medical

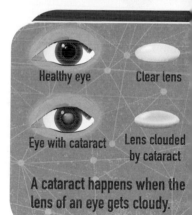

Healthy eye   Clear lens

Eye with cataract   Lens clouded by cataract

A cataract happens when the lens of an eye gets cloudy.

purpose. The Laserphaco Probe was a tool used during eye surgery to remove cataracts. Her probe used a laser, which was advanced for its time. It was less painful, more precise, and safer than earlier tools. Helping cataract patients see again has been one of Patricia's greatest joys.

Antonia Novello

"I want to be able to look back someday and say, 'I did make a difference.' Whether it was to open the minds of people to think that a woman can do a good job, or whether it's the fact that so many kids out there think that they could be like me." —Antonia Novello

As a child, Antonia Novello was often in pain and spent weeks every summer in a local hospital getting treatment. She suffered from a long-lasting illness that stopped her colon from working properly. Her condition could have been fixed with surgery, but her family didn't have enough money to travel to the surgical center. Finally, at ages 18 and 20, Antonia had the two surgeries that cured her. Her experience led her to a career in medicine— "I thought, when I grow up, no other person is going to wait 18 years for surgery," she said. Her career in medicine led her straight to the top!

Helping Kids

Antonia Novello was born in Puerto Rico in 1944 and attended both college and medical school there. She traveled to the University of

Antonia worked with others to help prevent childhood injury.

Michigan for nephrology (the study of the kidneys). Antonia chose this field because her favorite aunt had died of kidney failure. Antonia specialized in pediatric nephrology, taking care of young patients in Virginia. However, Antonia soon realized that she became too upset if her patients didn't get better. "When the pediatrician cries as much as the parents do, then you know it's time to get out," she said.

Antonia played an important role in starting the Healthy Children Ready to Learn initiative.

America's Doctor

Antonia went to work for the U.S. Public Health Service and helped draft national laws for organ transplants. In 1990, she became the first woman—and first Latina—to be appointed to U.S. Surgeon General, the most respected job in health care. During her time as Surgeon General, Antonia forced tobacco companies to change ads directed at children. She also focused attention on the problems of underage drinking, pediatric AIDS, women's health, and the problems minority groups had getting heath care. Later on, she worked for the United Nations Children's Fund (UNICEF) and the New York State Department of Health.

WHOA!

⚛ The Surgeon General is picked by the President of the United States!

⚛ Antonia taught Americans how to improve their health and lower their risk of getting sick.

> "I think there are two keys to being creatively productive. One is not being daunted by one's fear of failure. The second is sheer perseverance."
> —Mary-Claire King

What do you do when you have a hunch about something, but everyone says you're wrong? Do you give up? Mary-Claire King didn't. She had a hunch about cancer, and she followed it. And she was right!

Never Stop Doing Science

Mary-Claire King was born in 1946 in a suburb of Chicago. When she was in high school, she was heartbroken when one of her closest friends died from cancer. This sparked her interest in science. She graduated college with a math degree. When she was in graduate school, she took a course in genetics—the study of how different qualities, called traits, are passed down from parents to their children. Mary-Claire was fascinated. She changed her focus to genetics. But she couldn't get

Mary-Claire's research proved that the DNA of humans and chimps are 99 percent the same!

her experiments to work. She felt like a disaster in the lab. A professor told her, "If everyone whose experiments failed stopped doing science, there wouldn't be any science." Mary-Claire liked what she heard. Quickly, she switched into his lab, where she studied the genetic differences between chimpanzees and humans.

WHOA!

⚛ Researchers have since used Mary-Claire's methods to find out if other illnesses, such as Alzheimer's disease, are genetic, too.

⚛ Mary-Claire was awarded the important Lasker Prize in 2014.

Finding the Right Gene

Mary-Claire next turned her attention to breast cancer. Scientists thought that cancers were caused by viruses or from the environment. But Mary-Claire felt they could be inherited through genes. This meant it might be passed to family members, like inheriting blue eyes from your mother or brown hair from your father. She asked thousands of women with breast cancer about their family medical histories. She examined their chromosomes. Finally, Mary-Claire found a connection to a gene, called BRCA1. Her hunch was right! She was the first geneticist to show the link between breast cancer and a single gene. Her findings changed treatment and allowed women to find out early if they were at risk for getting the disease.

Mary-Claire received the National Medal of Science from President Barack Obama in May 2016.

Wafaa El-Sadr

"... the best thing one can do is to listen very carefully to what your patients are saying."

—Wafaa El-Sadr

In the early 1980s, Wafaa El-Sadr and her fellow doctors were puzzled when they read a report about the death of five men in New York City. How could they have all died from the same rare type of pneumonia? She didn't know it then, but Wafaa would become a pioneer in the treatment of a mysterious disease.

Mystery Sickness

Wafaa El-Sadr was born in 1950 in Egypt. She grew up in a family of doctors and wanted to be a doctor, too. She hoped to help cure diseases in poor countries around the world. After graduating medical school in Cairo, she traveled to the United States for more training. A few years later, a lot of people began getting a mysterious illness and dying. Nobody knew how to stop it. Wafaa left her job in Cleveland, Ohio, and moved to Harlem in New York City to take care of people—and to learn more about the disease. Later, she

This is an illustration of tuberculosis (also called TB). TB is an infection that affects the lungs.

and other doctors realized that a virus called HIV was making people's bodies weak. Patients who were no longer able to fight off infection had a condition called AIDS.

Curing with Care

Wafaa became the chief of the Division of Infectious Diseases at Harlem Hospital. She noticed that patients with AIDS often got tuberculosis, too. Then Wafaa discovered that most homeless and immigrant patients did not finish their tuberculosis medicine. They had no family or friends to help them through the six-month treatment.

Wafaa decided to change the way treatment clinics worked. She turned them into homey places that people enjoyed visiting every day. She trained and hired caring people who understood what patients were going through. The clinics became a support system for the patients. In one year, almost 95 percent of patients finished their treatment. Wafaa used the same homey-clinic idea to support HIV-positive mothers and children. Later, she would take on HIV treatment in Africa and Central Asia.

A red ribbon is the symbol for World AIDS Day. Every year on December 1, people can unite in the fight against HIV/AIDS and remember family and friends who have died.

WHOA!

❀ Wafaa has helped more than one million people complete their treatments and live healthier lives.

❀ In 2008, Wafaa was named a MacArthur Fellow for her ground-breaking response to the HIV and tuberculosis epidemics. This is often called "the genius award."

"You need a face to face the world."
—Maria Siemionow

Dr. Maria Siemionow's patient, Connie Culp, had lost the middle of her face to a shotgun blast. She couldn't breathe without a tube in her neck. She couldn't drink from a cup or taste or smell. Maria was about to perform the first near-total facial transplant. It was a difficult operation. A lot could go wrong. But Maria was prepared, and she was ready to give Connie a brand-new face.

Holding Hands

Maria Siemionow was born in Poland in 1950. Growing up, she and her family took summer trips throughout Europe. Maria was good at learning languages—and soon she was speaking five of them! Maria was good at science, too, and she was interested in medicine. She went to medical school in Poland and trained in hand surgery.

Microsurgery is a very detailed operation on a small area. A surgeon uses microscopes and small tools.

Maria traveled to different countries, working for "Physicians for Peace." She helped many children who had been in fires by operating on their burned hands. She couldn't do much for their burned faces at the time. Later, Maria wanted to focus on microsurgery and moved to the United States to train. In 1995, she became the director of Plastic Surgery Research and head of Microsurgery Training at the Cleveland Clinic. The memory of the burned children must have stayed with her, though. She made restoring damaged faces her next focus.

Face to Face

For many years, Maria studied exactly how a face transplant would be done. The skin on a face is thinner and trickier to work with than skin on hands. A face needs a nose, lips, and eyelids—and there aren't extras for people to donate. In 2008, Maria led a team of doctors in a 22-hour operation. She transplanted 80 percent of Connie Culp's face with the face of a woman who had recently died. Connie got an upper jaw, upper lip, cheeks, a nose, and eyelids. After the operation and recovery, Connie could breathe, speak, taste, smell, and eat on her own. Maria had literally put a new face on medicine!

WHOA!

- Maria has won many awards. She is considered a world leader in her field.

- Maria isn't only a surgeon. She's also a teacher *and* a research scientist.

- Maria is a photographer in her spare time. She loves taking pictures of people.

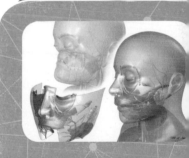

Connie has to take special medicine every day so that her body's immune system does not reject the new parts of her face. Maria is working on a way to adjust the immune system so that transplant patients will not have to take medicine.

Careers in Medicine

Are you curious about how things work? Do you like solving mysteries and helping people? Do you enjoy science? If you answered yes to these questions, a career in medicine may be perfect for you! Here are some to think about:

⚛ **Doctors (MDs)** are licensed to treat patients. They examine patients, identify illnesses, prescribe medicine, order diagnostic tests, and may perform surgery. You can be a general doctor or choose a specialty, such as:

Cardiologist: treats the heart

Dermatologist: treats the skin

Gastroenterologist: treats the digestive system

ENT specialist: treats the ears, nose, and throat

Neurologist: treats the brain and nervous system

Obstetrician: treats women during pregnancy and childbirth

Oncologist: treats patients with cancer

Ophthalmologist: treats eyes

Orthopedist: treats bones

Pediatrician: treats babies and children

Psychiatrist: treats patients with mental disorders

Surgeon: operates on patients

School needed	college plus 4 years of medical school and 3-8 years of residency.
What you can do now	help care for family and pets, volunteer at a hospital, interview your doctor, take part in science experiments, play with puzzles

✸ **Registered nurses (RNs)** work closely with doctors and help treat patients. They also oversee patient recovery, and counsel on healthy habits and after-hospital treatment.

School needed	college with a degree in nursing
What you can do now	help take care of family members and pets, volunteer at a hospital, do science experiments, practice being a good listener

✸ **Physical therapists (PTs)** treat patients by teaching them exercises that strengthen and stretch muscles and lessen pain.

School needed	college plus a graduate degree in physical therapy
What you can do now	play sports (you'll need strength), learn about the bones and muscles in the human body

✸ **Medical scientists** have different specialties. Chemists, physicists, geneticists, and molecular biologists are all types of medical scientists. They research viruses and bacteria that cause disease so they can develop new vaccines and medications. They also use high-powered microscopes to understand how human genes work.

School needed	college plus a graduate degree in science or medicine
What you can do now	take part in science experiments, learn to use a microscope, visit science museums, learn to code

Glossary

Alzheimer's disease: a progressive disease that destroys memory and other important mental functions.

anesthesiology: The practice of medicine dedicated to preventing the feeling of pain.

cancer: Disease caused by an uncontrolled division of abnormal cells in a part of the body.

chemistry: The study of matter and the changes that take place with that matter.

chemotherapy: The use of drugs to destroy cancer cells.

chromosomes: Thread-like strands inside human cells that carry genetic information.

colon: The main part of your large intestine.

DNA: DNA stands for deoxyribonu cleic acid. It is what genes are made of. It holds the code for every cell in your body.

Down syndrome: A condition in which a person is born with an extra 21st chromosome. The extra chromosome causes delays in mental and physical development.

dyslexia: A learning disorder characterized by difficulty reading.

epidemic: A disease that spreads rapidly among many people at the same time.

hormone: A substance made in the body that helps regulate cells and tissues.

immune disorder: A condition in which the body's immune system does not work properly.

immune system: The body's defense against infections and other harmful invaders.

infectious disease: A disorder caused by organisms such as bacteria, viruses, fungi, or parasites.

influenza: Also called "the flu," an infectious disease caused by an influenza virus that affects the nose, throat, and lungs.

insulin: A hormone that helps your body turn sugar into energy.

kidneys: The organs that filter your blood, removing wastes and extra water, released in the form of urine.

leukemia: Cancer of the blood cells.

malaria: A blood disease transmitted by mosquitoes.

measles: A highly contagious virus with a high fever and rash, spread by coughing and sneezing.

microsurgery: Intricate surgery performed using miniaturized instruments and a microscope.

Nobel Prize: The most prestigious international award given for amazing inventions and discoveries or contributions to society.

organ transplant: A surgical operation in which a failing or damaged organ is removed and replaced with a functioning one.

pediatrician: A doctor who takes care of babies and children.

physics: The study of the interaction between matter and energy.

plastic surgery: Surgery that restores, reconstructs, or changes the appearance of the human body.

pneumonia: A lung infection that causes inflammation in your lungs' air sacs, or alveoli, filling them with fluid or pus, making it difficult to breathe.

residency: A stage of advanced medical training in a hospital where doctors learn more about specific medical treatments.

smallpox: A contagious viral disease, with fever and round blisters (pox) usually leaving permanent scars.

tuberculosis: An infectious disease that usually affects the lungs.

Index